Van Gogh and his letters

# VAN GOGH

## and his letters

Leo Jansen

VAN GOGH MUSEUM

schetsje het zwart 't donkerst is zitten de g
in de aquarel. — Donkergroen bru
. Nu adieu, en geloof me dat sommi
zelf om lach dat de lui mij die eige
is ben dan een vriend van de natuur
n werk — ook van menschen vooral
rse kwaadaardigheden en absurditeiten waaro
u op mijn hoofd denkt. Enfin — tot
handdruk. b a t. Vincent

THE LEGACY OF VINCENT VAN GOGH was not just a great number of beautiful paintings and drawings but also the most fascinating artist's correspondence that we know. Great artists have been inspired by the wealth of artistic and philosophical ideas expressed in his letters, and writers have placed these moving *documents humains* in the front rank of world literature. For more than a century, readers and art lovers have been swept away by the story of this rebel and seeker.

During Van Gogh's lifetime (1853-1890), there were a few people in his immediate circle who already recognised the originality of his ideas and his ability to express them in a distinctive way. Within three years of his death, long excerpts from his letters began to appear in *Mercure de France*, the leading French journal of art and literature. A German translation of these excerpts was made, and thousands of copies of this were sold in the first decade of the twentieth century. The publication in 1914 of a three-volume edition of Van Gogh's *Brieven aan zijn broeder* (Letters to his brother) finally made most of the letters written by this pioneering painter accessible to a large audience.

1
Letter to Theo, detail
The Hague,
c. 1 August 1882
(253/221)
Van Gogh Museum,
Amsterdam

2
The first letter written
by Vincent to Theo
The Hague,
29 September 1872
(1/1)
Van Gogh Museum,
Amsterdam
The upper left-hand
corner is torn off,
but the salutation
must have been
'my dear Theo'
('Waarde Theo').

Vincent van Gogh was a complex personality with wide-ranging ideas, so that anyone seeking to become acquainted with him must delve into his letters – and read and reread them. This is why 'Van Gogh the letter-writer' is the focal point of this book. There is no better way to approach the artist than by examining his letters, scrutinising both their meaning and their appearance down to the last detail.

## EXCEPTIONAL LETTERS

It is a comforting thought that the perishable letters of a great nineteenth-century artist should have withstood the ravages of time, although this is not exceptional: letters have also survived from such contemporaries and friends of Van Gogh as Paul Gauguin, Camille and Lucien Pissarro, and Henri de Toulouse-Lautrec. Their letters are interesting because of the light they shed on their circumstances and artistic ambitions, but they do not have the fascinating quality of Van Gogh's letters. What is it that explains the magic of Van Gogh the letter-writer?

Such questions never have simple answers. To begin with, Van Gogh's life story is clearly unique. The letters, which bear first-hand witness to his life, necessarily tell an autobiographical story: a dozen occupations and even more failures during his wanderings through the Netherlands, England, Belgium and France; the religious zeal and *imitatio Christi* that obsessed him for several years; the realisation of his artistic calling at the age of twenty-seven; the fight to master pen and brush while alienating himself from everyone around him; the astonishing artistic metamorphosis he experienced in Paris; and, finally, the periods of mental instability and depression that plagued him during the years preceding his suicide.

Van Gogh, moreover, was a born writer. He may have struggled to learn to draw and paint, but he had an innate talent for writing. A great many of his letters are about art – his own and that of others – yet he also thought deeply about metaphysical and ethical issues and reflected at length on human behaviour and social developments. He wrote about such subjects in an infectious way, immediately drawing his readers into the world of his

Theo,

Dank voor je brief,
het deed mij genoegen dat je
weer goed aangekomen zijt.
Ik heb je de eerste dagen ge-
mist & het was mij vreemd
je niet te vinden als ik 'smid-
dags thuis kwam.
Wij hebben prettige dagen sa-
men gehad, en tusschen de
droppeltjes door toch nog al
eens gewandeld & het een en
ander gezien.
Wat vreesselijk weer, je zult
het wel benauwd hebben
op je wandelingen naar
Oisterwijk. Gisteren is het hard-
draverij geweest ter gelegenheid van
de tentoonstelling, maar de illumi-
natie & het vuurwerk zijn uit-
gesteld, om het slechte weer, het
is dus maar goed dat je niet
gebleven zijt om die te zien. Groeten
van de familie Haanebeek & Roos.
Steeds je liefh. Vincent

life and thought. He used the evocative and direct language of a strong personality. He often felt, rightly or wrongly, that he was undervalued and badly treated. Virtually every reader can recognise these sentiments, as well as such recurrent themes as a lack of money, loneliness and the need for love. It may seem paradoxical, but Van Gogh's extremely personal correspondence rises above the individual to achieve the universality of great literature.

The original letters, then, bring the writer very close to us, as we see not only how his handwriting changed over the years but also how it could vary within a single letter. At times we witness Van Gogh's violent mood swings, betrayed by the words and lines he added – or crossed out – as well as by underlinings and emphasis in the writing. And nothing is more symbolic of the artist's voice than the many beautiful sketches he made to show the recipients of his letters what he was working on.

**THE EARLY YEARS**

'My dear Theo': these are the simple, familiar words with which Vincent van Gogh's correspondence began in September 1872 (2). Hundreds of letters were to follow, in which Vincent confided in his brother Theo, sharing his experiences and reporting what he had seen or read. As the youngest trainee of the internationally active French art dealer Goupil, Vincent spent four years at the branch in The Hague, followed by some three years alternating between London and Paris (3). Works of art formed part of his everyday environment, and he was also an ardent visitor to museums. In July 1873 he wrote from London: 'English art did not appeal to me much at first, one has to get used to it. There are some good painters here, however, including Millais, who made "The Huguenot", Ophelia, &c. – of which you probably know the engraved versions – that is very beautiful. Then Boughton, of whom you know the "Puritans going to Church" in our Galerie photographique. I have seen very beautiful things by him. Moreover, among the old painters, Constable, a landscape painter who lived around 30 years ago, whose work is splendid, something like Diaz and Daubigny. And Reynolds

and Gainsborough, who mostly painted very, very beautiful portraits of women, and then Turner, after whom you have probably seen engravings. Several good French painters live here, including Tissot, after whom there are various photos in our Galerie photographique, Otto Weber and Heilbuth. The last one is currently making dazzlingly beautiful paintings in the style of Linder.' Another letter contains a long list of painters he particularly liked (4).

An avid reader, Van Gogh was equally enthusiastic about literature. Impressions of books he had read, advice to Theo on what to read and poems copied out of books all appear time and again in his letters. He cannot refrain from urging Theo to read the same things that he reads, writing in August 1874: 'Buy Alphonse Karr's "Voyage autour de mon jardin" with the money I gave you. Be sure to do so, I want you to read it.'

At times his eagerness is accompanied by fatherly exhortations to his younger brother, and this characterises the roles they assumed in their early years: 'You must in any case go to the museum often, it's good to be acquainted with the old painters, too, & if you get the chance, read about

Ik schrijf hieronder enkele
namen van schilders van
wie ik bizonder veel houdt.
Scheffer, Delaroche, Hébert
Hamon
Leys, Tissot, Lagye Boughton
Millais, Thys Maris, de Groux
de Braekeleer Jr.
Millet, Jules Breton, Feyen-Perrin
Eugène Feyen, Brion Jundt
George Saal, Israels Anker
Knaus, Vautier, Jourdan
Jalabert, Antigna, Compte-Calix
Rochussen, Meissonier, Zamacois
Madrazzo, Ziem, Boudin
Gerome, Fromentin, de Tournemine
Passini

Decamps, Bonnington, Diaz
Th. Rousseau, Troyon, Dupré
Paul Huet, Corot, Schreyer
Jacque, Otto Weber, Daubigny
Wahlberg, Bernier, Emile Breton
Chenu, Cesar de Cocq, Mlle Collart
Bodmer, Koekkoek, Schelfhout,
Weissenbruch & last not least
Maris & Mauve
Maar ik zou zoo door kunnen
gaan, ik wiet niet hoe lang,

art and especially magazines about art, the Gazette des Beaux-Arts &c. When there's an opportunity I'll send you a book by Bürger about the museums of The Hague & Amsterdam; when you've finished it there will be an opportunity to send it back to me.'

4
Letter to Theo
London, January 1874
(17/13)
Van Gogh Museum,
Amsterdam

It was also at this period that he wrote of his profound love of nature and landscape, as he spent hours taking long walks outside the city. He had to manage this in London as best he could: 'I walk here as much as I can, but I'm very busy. It's absolutely beautiful here (even though it's in the city). There are lilacs & hawthorns & laburnums &c. blossoming in all the gardens, & the chestnut trees are magnificent. If one truly loves nature, one finds beauty everywhere. Yet I sometimes yearn so much for Holland & especially Helvoirt.'

Thus the letters of the young Van Gogh paint a picture of his intellectual self-education, and the way he used art and literature both to discover and to define himself – and it is essential to know this if we are to understand him later as an artist.

When Theo started work at Goupil's three years after Vincent, the devoted brothers became true companions in arms. They had the same interests, but we are unsure of Theo's part in the exchange of correspondence; almost none of the letters he wrote to his brother before 1888 have survived. Truly intimate subjects, such as 'the question of women' (how young men should behave towards the female sex, and what they expected of marriage and their future wives), were too sensitive to commit to paper; at most they were touched upon briefly and subsequently discussed in private when they met at their parents' house, as they often did at Christmas. In October 1874 Vincent wrote: 'It will surely be winter soon, how fortunate that Christmas is in the winter, that's why I like winter better than any other season, Christmas and New Year's Eve are even better than the autumn. How wonderful it will be to sail down the Thames and across the sea, and then those friendly Dutch dunes and that small tower that one already sees from a great distance. How little we see of each other, old boy, and how little we see of our parents.' That nostalgia for the warmth of home is expressed

again and again in Vincent's early letters and it returned later on, in the form of undisguised childhood recollections, when he attempted to work from memory in the south of France (5).

## HARD TIMES

'There is quiet melancholy, certainly, thank God, but I don't know if we're allowed to feel it yet, you see I say *we*, I no more than you. Pa wrote to me recently, "Melancholy does not hurt, but makes us see things with a holier eye." *That* is true "quiet melancholy", fine gold, but we aren't that far yet, not by a long way. Let us hope & pray that we may come so far.' In 1874-75 the tone of his letters became increasingly gloomy, marking the prelude to the religious period of the twenty-year-old Van Gogh, who was dismissed from his job at Goupil's in the spring of 1876. While he investigated a variety of possibilities in his search for some form of employment – going from bookseller's employee to assistant teacher to evangelist – biblical allusions and quotations became more and more frequent in his letters. The words

And thou too, whosoe'er thou art
That readest this brief psalm
As one by one thy hopes depart
Be resolute and calm.

O, fear not in a world like this
And thou shalt know ere long
Know, how sublime a thing it is
To suffer and be strong. —

As being sorrowful yet always rejoicing
Als droevig zynde maar altijd blyde

After years of city toil
I hear the old church bells
They sing a strange new song
Whilst the old song in my memory dwells.
A strange new song, with strange new words
That many sorrows bring
And sorrowful I once again
I will rejoice at what they sing.

Het kind vertrouwt zich aan zyn Vader
Dat is die Vader waard. —
uw Vader toch wien hebt gy nader
In Hemel of op aard.

On this man will I look, saith the Lord, even on
him that is poor and needy and sorrowful and
that trembleth at My word. —

En Hij ging in het midden
van hen door en zeide Myne
ure is nog niet gekomen. —

Vader wy bidden U niet dat Gy ons uit de wereld wegneemt maar dat
Gy ons bewaart voorden booze. —
De Heer is uw bewaarder de Heer is uwe schaduw aan uwe regterhand
De Heer is niet verre van een iegelyk onzer.
Als één lid lydt dan lijden alle leden mede. — Verbind Gij o Heer
ons innig aan elkaar en laat de Liefde tot U dien band meer en
meer versterken. —
En Mozes nam den staf Gods in de hand. —
De duivel is nooit zoo zwart of men kan hem nog wel onder de
oogen zien. —

In het konimkryk der Hemelen trouwen zy niet
en worden zy niet ten huwelyk gegeven. In Christus is
noch man noch vrouw maar Hy is alles en in allen

Dezelfde mond die sprak "wees oprecht als de duiven" liet er ook

'sorrowful, yet alway rejoicing', from the second epistle of St Paul to the Corinthians, became his personal motto, occurring in his letters in both Dutch and English (6). The same shift can be seen in his reading, and he became more enthusiastic than ever about the religious paintings of Ary Scheffer, particularly *Christus consolator* (7), prints of which he acquired to hang in his room and to present as gifts to members of his family.

Van Gogh's father, himself a minister, thought his son's religious zeal excessive, and one of his sisters called him a 'compulsive churchgoer'. Vincent peppered his letters with passages from the Bible, prayer books and hymnals. 'Do you ever go to The Lord's Supper? They that be whole need not a physician, but they that are sick. [...] Don't be afraid, when you're out walking in the evening and there is no one near by, to sing a psalm: "The panting hart the hunt escaped", or "O why art thou cast down, my soul?" or "Centre of our longing" or "I know in Whom my faith is founded". The years between 20 and 30 are full of all sorts of dangers, full of great danger, yea, the danger of sin and death, but also full of light and God's comfort. Wrestling, you will emerge victorious, and when they're over you will think back on them with nostalgia and say, it was a good time after all.'

His religious fanaticism caused Van Gogh to drift further and further away from his friends and family. The distance between them became physical as well as emotional when Vincent moved at the end of 1878 to the Borinage, a poor mining district in Belgium where he lived in abject poverty. The handful of reluctant letters from that period speak volumes: Vincent, who felt that his family had abandoned him and that he had no prospects, reached an impasse. In the meantime, he had turned his back on everything even remotely connected with 'official' religion or the church. Worse still, he had become estranged from Theo. A low ebb in their relations is documented in the opening of a long letter that Vincent wrote to Theo in the early summer of 1880, when he was struggling to escape his hopeless situation in the Borinage: 'My dear Theo, I am writing to you with some reluctance, not having done so in such a long time, for many reasons. To a certain degree you have become a stranger to me, and I have become the same to you, more than you may think; perhaps it would be better for us not to continue in this way. I should probably not have written to you even now if I were not obliged and did not feel the need to do so, if you yourself had not given me cause. At Etten I learned that you had sent 50 francs for me; well, I have accepted them. Certainly with reluctance, certainly with a rather melancholy feeling, but I am in a kind of cul-de-sac or mess. How can I do otherwise? So I am writing to you to thank you. Perhaps you know that I am back in the Borinage. Pa would prefer that I stay in the neighbourhood of Etten; I refused, and in this I believe I acted for the best. I have unwittingly become more or less a kind of impossible and suspect personage in the family, at least somebody in whom they have no confidence, so how could I possibly be of use to anyone? Therefore, above all, I think the best and most reasonable thing for me to do is to go away and keep at a convenient distance, so that I cease to exist for you all.' Later he referred to this dark period as 'a few years which I find hard to understand myself, when I was confused by religious ideas – by a sort of mysticism'.

All the same, letter-writing took on a new meaning in this period, possibly for the very reason that he was struggling with himself and with the traditions in which he had been brought up. When everything was going well for him, his letters were little more than a means of communication, a way of exchanging news and ideas. From 1877 onwards, however, it became obvious that he was equally motivated by the urge to formulate and develop his own notions and thoughts, and that writing had become an end in itself. Before this time his letters had been relatively short, but now they became considerably longer, and he adopted a much more characteristic, more didactic style. The letters, in short, became an integral part of Van Gogh's quest.

## THE EMERGING ARTIST

The crisis years ended in the summer of 1880, when Van Gogh emerged rather suddenly from his cocoon of uncertainty and despair. At Theo's suggestion Vincent resolved to become a draughtsman or illustrator, hoping to work for illustrated magazines, which were increasing dramatically in number and popularity. From this time on, the letters represent the written complement to his artistic career.

For a long time Van Gogh followed in the artistic footsteps of Jean-François Millet and Jules Breton, who had portrayed poor, humble French peasants in an idealised way (8). One utterance (of many) says enough: 'Millet is: PÈRE Millet, namely a counsellor and guide in *everything* for the younger painters.' From the artists of the Hague School Van Gogh derived the sobriety of the landscape and a greyish, rather sombre palette. It was Anton Mauve, a leading exponent of this movement, who taught Van Gogh the rudiments of painting (9).

Because of Theo's financial support, Vincent felt obliged to make regular progress reports, and he was also eager to hear his brother's opinion. He pursued his self-education as an artist in the way he had always done everything – uninterruptedly and with a passion sometimes bordering on obsession. 'At the moment I'm working on no fewer than

8
Jules Breton,
*Women gleaning*, 1868
The Metropolitan
Museum of Art,
New York
Bequest of
Collis P. Huntington

9
Anton Mauve,
*Fishing boat on
the beach*, 1882
Gemeentemuseum,
The Hague

10
Sketch in a
letter to Theo
The Hague, c. 27 June
1883 (359/296)
Van Gogh Museum,
Amsterdam

11
Vincent van Gogh,
*Head of a woman*,
1882-83
Van Gogh Museum,
Amsterdam

12
Letter to Theo
Drenthe, 28 October
1883 (401/336)
Van Gogh Museum,
Amsterdam

7 or 8 drawings, around 1 metre in size, so you can imagine how swamped I am with work. But I hope so much to make my hand more skilful through this period of drudgery. My dislike of working with charcoal, for instance, grows less every day. This is because I've found a way to fix the charcoal and to work over it, with printer's ink, for example. Here you have a little scratch of potato diggers, though in the drawing they are slightly farther apart.' This is followed by a little sketch of the drawing in question (10).

Making an all-out effort was not enough for Van Gogh. Each and every letter from the early 1880s testifies to his single-minded enthusiasm and his total immersion in art: his own work as well as the paintings, drawings and prints of others. He practised incessantly with pencil and brush, 'scarcely taking time even to eat or drink,' and he walked for miles through the surrounding countryside, in search of landscapes and characteristic figures to depict (12). He soon wanted to

18

om een half jaar moedeloosheid te veroorzaken
waarna men toch eindelijk ziet dat men niet zich
had moeten laten desorienteeren –
Van twee personen ken ik den zielstrijd tusschen
het ik ben schilder en het ik ben geen schilder.
van Rappard en van mij zelf – een strijd soms bang
een strijd die juist is dat wat het onderscheid is tusschen
ons en zekere anderen die minder serieus het opnemen
voor ons zelf hebben wij het soms verweerd aan 't eind
eener melankolie een beetje licht een beetje vooruitgang
zekere anderen hebben minder strijd dat ~~hen~~ ook hun
misschien makkelijker ook het ~~niet~~ persoonlijk
karakter ontwikkelt zich ook minder. Zij ~~zouden~~ ook
dien strijd hebben en ik zeg weet van uw zelf dat gij
het gevaar om door lui die zonder twijfel magere beste
intenties hebben van streek te worden gebragt –
Als als en u zelf zegt u Gij zijt geen schilder – schilder
dan juist Kerel en die hem bedaart ook maar
slechts daardoor – Wie als hy dat voelt gaat naar
vrienden en zijn nood klaagt verliest iets van
zijn mannelijkheid iets van het beste wat in hem is –
Uw vrienden kunnen slechts zijn dezulken die
zich daartegen vechten door eigen voorbeeld van
actie ~~hij~~ active in te opwekken –

work in colour, and he discussed the saleability of his work with Theo: 'Whatever you do, do not suspect me of indifference towards earning money, for I mean to take the shortest route to that end. Provided it leads to real and lasting earnings, which I see for myself only in the future if something truly good comes of my work, not by working exclusively at saleability – which one must pay for later – but by studying nature sincerely [...]. But if you were to say, "work on those forest scenes or landscapes or marines", it would not necessarily prevent greater and more serious things and I would have nothing against it. I'd only want to know that they are worth the brushes, the paint and the canvas, and that it is not throwing away money to make a lot of them, and that their sale would cover the cost of making them.'

Theo had meanwhile been appointed to the influential position of manager of Goupil's Paris branch, and Vincent hoped that this would provide a means to create interest in his own work. However, it was a long time – too long, in Vincent's opinion – before Theo found his work good enough to promote. The brothers experienced several discordant interludes, especially in 1882, when Vincent decided to live with the prostitute Sien Hoornik (11) – an episode in which he finally enjoyed some measure of domestic comfort – and again when he tried to persuade his brother to give up his reputable position in Paris to become a painter like himself. Vincent refused to consider the obvious financial drawbacks, and brushed aside Theo's doubts as to whether he had enough talent: 'In my view it would be an error of judgement if you were to continue in business in Paris. So the conclusion, two brothers, painters. Whether it's in your nature? You could occupy yourself struggling hard and fruitlessly against nature precisely by doubting whether you can, and thus hamper your own liberation. Unfortunately, I know all about that.' Needless to say, Vincent's plan lacked all sense of reality. This episode was one of the most telling as regards Van Gogh's single-mindedness and egocentricity – for these, too, were strong character traits of his, which were to lead to many conflicts.

## THE FRENCH YEARS

Van Gogh's so-called Dutch years, which can be considered his period of training, came to an end in late 1885, when he moved to Paris after a short stay in Antwerp. As soon as he moved in with his brother in March 1886, the need to write instantly disappeared. This explains the scarcity of letters from 1886-87 – a great pity, since it was at this time that he underwent his de-

13

Eugène Delacroix,

*Christ on the Sea*

*of Galilee,* 1853

The Metropolitan

Museum of Art, New York

H.O. Havemeyer

Collection

cisive artistic transformation. In the Louvre he looked carefully at the work of Eugène Delacroix, whose theory of colour he had already studied in artists' manuals in the Netherlands and whose *Christ on the Sea of Galilee* he had described as 'brilliant' (13). Van Gogh got to know the Parisian avant-garde and made friends who included Emile Bernard, Paul Signac and Henri de Toulouse-Lautrec (14). He joined their ranks and managed to make fundamental changes to his palette. Unfortunately, much of his life in those crucial years remains veiled in mystery.

It was not until the spring of 1888, when he travelled to Arles in the south of France, that the correspondence regained its former intensity. The letters from this period show that Van Gogh had matured in many ways. Although still an inveterate seeker, he had become artistically more adult and self-assured. Moreover, his relations with Theo were on a more equal footing, the earlier tensions having given way to mutual understanding and solidarity.

The essence of Vincent's artistic programme can be summarised in two words: colour and portraiture – although in fact he mainly painted landscapes during his time in Arles: 'I want to do figures, figures & more figures, it's stronger than me, this series of bipeds from the baby to Socrates and from the black-haired woman with white skin to the woman with yellow hair and a sunburnt face the colour of brick. Meanwhile, I mostly do other things.'

He was also preoccupied with the renewal of art and the possibilities for collaboration between artists. The mounting tension and strained expectations as the time approached when Gauguin would move into the Yellow House (15, 16), the great effort Van Gogh made to furnish the house and decorate it with a series of paintings in readiness for the great master – all this is vividly recounted in the letters (17). Gauguin, who arrived in Arles at the end of October 1888, left town after only two months, following a violent outburst: their temperaments were psychologically and artistically incompatible (18).

This ushered in a period of disappointment when Van Gogh was plagued by episodes of mental instability. At first he went several times for treatment

14
Henri de Toulouse-
Lautrec,
*Portrait of Vincent
van Gogh*, 1887
Van Gogh Museum,
Amsterdam

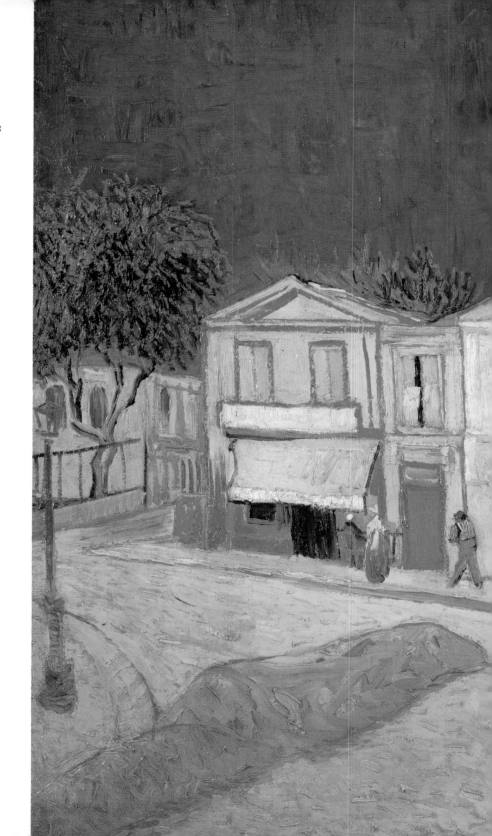

15
Vincent van Gogh,
*The Yellow House*, 1888
Van Gogh Museum,
Amsterdam

to the local hospital, but in May 1889 he had himself admitted voluntarily
to the psychiatric clinic at nearby Saint-Rémy. The tone of the letters now
becomes more sombre: Van Gogh was losing his old resilience and viewed
his efforts at painting as insignificant, despite the fact that he had begun
to make a name for himself among both artists and art critics. In March 1889
he wrote to his brother: 'Sometimes moods of indescribable mental
anguish, sometimes moments when the veil of time and the fatality of

circumstances seemed to be lifted for an instant. Of course you are right after all, damn well right – even if you are set on hoping, one probably has to accept the disastrous reality.' Ten months and several breakdowns later, he wrote: 'After all, this much is certain: what is important is not playing the part of a proud man or having great hopes for the future. Let's take the terrible realities for what they are, and if it is necessary for me to give up painting, I think I should do so.' Reading the letters from this last period is an experience at once moving and heart-rending, because we witness in painful proximity the alternating depressions and flickerings of hope. It is all the more distressing because we know how the story ends: Van Gogh's return to the countryside near Paris failed to heal his mind; on 27 July 1890 he shot himself in the chest in the fields of Auvers-sur-Oise and died two days later, with Theo at his side.

## THE CORRESPONDENTS

Since Theo (19) was for years Vincent's great confidant, and most of the surviving letters are addressed to him, it is easy to get the impression that Van Gogh never wrote to anyone else and that he himself never received any letters. Nothing could be further from the truth. The list of extant letters includes some 820 letters written by Van Gogh, of which approximately 650 are addressed to Theo (see p. 81). Thus there are roughly 170 known letters written to others. These cast Van Gogh in roles other than that of brother, and they show that he geared not only his tone and style but also his frame of reference (examples and comparisons, for instance) to the recipients of his letters. If we confine ourselves to his years as an artist – the decade from 1880 to 1890 – three correspondents merit special mention.

The letters written to Anthon van Rappard (1858-1892) during the period 1881-85 contain a splendid sampling of the artistic notions Van Gogh entertained during his years of training and of the artistic obstacles he sought to overcome. Van Rappard was a young Dutch painter who met Van Gogh in the autumn of 1880 in the artistic circle surrounding the art academy at Brussels, just when Van Gogh had decided to attempt a career in art (20).

20
Portrait photograph
of Anthon van
Rappard, c. 1880
Van Gogh Museum,
Amsterdam

21
List of prints in
a letter to Anthon
van Rappard
The Hague,
c. 18 January 1883
(303/R22)
Van Gogh Museum,
Amsterdam

> 22
Vincent van Gogh,
*The potato eaters*, 1885
Van Gogh Museum,
Amsterdam

Theo was probably responsible for bringing the two together. For the next five years Van Rappard would be the only artist friend with whom Van Gogh could continually exchange ideas about the profession of painting, especially its technical aspects. The two friends had only just set out on their respective paths, but Van Rappard had a much more academic orientation than the individualistic Van Gogh, and this led to fascinating and at times vehement discussions in their letters. 'I won't go into generalities about technique, but I do foresee that, precisely when I become stronger than I am at this moment in what I shall call *power of expression*, people will say, not *less* but in fact *even more* than now, that I have *no* technique. Consequently, I am in complete agreement with you that I must say even *more forcibly* what I am saying in my present work – and I am toiling away to strengthen myself in this respect – but that the general public will understand me better *then* – no. [...] *One* MUST therefore *work* on technique in so far as one must say what one feels better, more accurately, more profoundly, but – with the less verbiage the better. But the rest – one need not occupy oneself with it.' Van

Ik heb van Percy Macquoid een
meisjeskopje, dat prachtig mooi is, gevonden
eene toulmer naar een schildery van hem
andere mooie bladen ~~~~ die ik sedert vond zyn o.a.
Constant.        Fellahs malades au bord du N.
Julien Dupré        Gardeuse de vaches
Smith —        A street in South Lambeth
Ridley                Boatrace.
Robinson        A street in ~~~~ Whitechapel
Green .
Regamey        Prison in New York
Thulstrup /        Workroom in Sailors hospital or hom.
Abbey                Wintergirl
   "                Peter Stuyvesant
Reinhardt        Fishermen.
Barnard                6 bladen
Ed. frère        Woodgatherers
Buchmann        donkeys on Hampsteadheath
   "                Guttering poppies
Waller        Pip girls (Charbonniers)

31

Gogh and Van Rappard shared a passion for the prints they found in illustrated magazines; they regularly sent each other rolls containing prints, and made lists of what they had bought (21). Their letters show Van Gogh as both enthusiastic and tiresome, and one is hardly surprised to read that Van Rappard called him a 'zealot'. Their correspondence ended shortly after

Van Rappard said of Van Gogh's masterpiece *The potato eaters* that it was 'superficial' and 'indifferent' and 'not meant seriously' (22).

The letters written to Emile Bernard (1868-1941) in the period 1886-89, are – like the letters to Van Rappard – a typical artists' correspondence (23), in which Van Gogh, having meanwhile become more mature and chastened, constantly aired his ideas about art, literature and life, clearly with the intention of keeping Bernard – a fiercely ambitious painter-poet who

was fifteen years his junior – on the right path. To this end, Van Gogh wrote to him in a deliberately casual tone, occasionally using strong language encountered nowhere else in his letters. After expounding upon the importance of sound nutrition, he went on to say: 'And now you'll perhaps tell me that I'm bloody well getting on your nerves. That you want to go to the brothel, and that you don't give a damn about all the rest. My word, that depends, but I can't say other than that. Art is long and life is short, and we must wait patiently while trying to sell our skin dearly. [...] in order to do good work you have to eat well, be well housed, shag from time to time, smoke your pipe and drink your coffee in peace.'

Van Gogh believed in Bernard's talent and spoke very highly of one of his still lifes, which he actually imitated to some extent (24, 25). Fortunately, Bernard had a mind of his own. He evidently had no qualms about contradicting Van Gogh, goading him all the more into making pedantic observations. A particular aspect of Van Gogh's letters to Emile Bernard – 22 are known, the last of which dates from 1889 – is that they frequently discuss the sacrifices an artist must make to allow his art to reach maturity: he is bound to be solitary and misunderstood by society and has to subordinate his love life to his creativity; putting every bit of his energy into his art, he wears himself down both mentally and physically. If the picture of the romantic artist is confirmed anywhere, it is in these letters.

Van Rappard and Bernard were fellow painters. By contrast, the letters Vincent wrote to his sister Willemien (1862-1941), who was nine years younger, are more everyday and intimate in tone (26). In the 23 extant letters from the years 1887-90, he seems to want to prepare her for 'real' life. His own disappointments resound with regularity. Wil, as he called her, had literary aspirations, and Vincent, who was older and wiser, warned her repeatedly of the great sacrifices demanded by art and the isolation to which it could lead. Every letter contains suggested reading, or discusses such things as the essence of modern art. Typically, one of the letter sketches he chose to send her shows his painting *Woman reading a novel* (61, 62).

Vincent advised Wil to seek refuge in everyday life and to let it be a source of inspiration when writing: 'And above all I find it a very worrying matter that you believe you have to study in order to write. No, my dear little sister, learn to dance or fall in love with one or more notary's clerks, officers, in short whoever's within your reach; rather, much rather commit any number of follies than study in Holland, it serves absolutely no purpose other than to make someone dull, and so I won't hear of it.' The letters to Wil also betray the homesickness for Holland that Van Gogh felt in the years after his breakdown, and it is remarkable that he fell back on authors who had engaged his attention earlier, such as Dickens and Shakespeare. The desire for intimacy and security resonating in the letters to Wil says much about Van Gogh's state of mind.

## INEVITABLE LOSSES

The Van Goghs were a close-knit family who attached great importance to strong ties of kinship and family and mutual solidarity. From the moment that Vincent went to work at the age of sixteen for an art dealer in The Hague, far away from safe, familiar Zundert, he must have written to his parents at least once a week. Later, when Theo followed in his footsteps and their sisters went to boarding schools or became lady-companions, the family wrote a great many letters, frequently containing such words of encouragement as 'do write again soon' or 'I'm longing for a letter from you' – often accompanied by a 'handshake in thought'. In that period Vincent alone must have written and received hundreds more letters than we now know. The later correspondence and family papers also contain reports of letters sent or received. If every recipient had saved Van Gogh's letters, and if he had not thrown away any of the ones he received, the correspondence might have numbered well over 2,000 letters.

We will never know exactly how many letters have been lost, but we have Vincent's brother Theo to thank for the fact that so many letters by the then unknown artist have survived: Theo, as it happens, seems to have saved almost everything. When he died in January 1891 – only six months after

Vincent – his widow, Jo van Gogh-Bonger (27), found in a cupboard around 650 letters that Vincent had written to Theo between September 1872 and July 1890. In 1914 she published these letters as *Brieven aan zijn broeder* (Letters to his brother), complete with a full introduction – a milestone for the biography of Van Gogh. Approximately 95 per cent of Van Gogh's surviving letters are now preserved in the collection of the Van Gogh Museum.

Theo was, in fact, Vincent's only true and lifelong friend. That the brothers' intensive correspondence was a yardstick of their devotion to one another was a fact noticed by Jo when she became Theo's wife: in the fifteen months between their wedding day and Vincent's death, Jo saw more than sixty of the familiar yellow envelopes from Arles, Saint-Rémy and Auvers-sur-Oise land on the doormat of their Paris flat.

It is fascinating to think that in the desk drawers or attics of the descendants of Van Gogh's correspondents there could still be bundles of letters waiting to be discovered. The chance of this is small, however, since Van Gogh has been world-famous for nearly a century and his letters are just as highly valued as his drawings and paintings. We may therefore assume that all those connected in the slightest way with his life, either directly or indirectly, have already undertaken a thorough search of their old papers. Fortunately, though, surprises are always possible: in 2001 an unknown letter unexpectedly came to light that the young Van Gogh had written to a man who played an important role in the literary and artistic education of the Van Gogh brothers: H.G. Tersteeg, the head of Goupil's branch in The Hague. Vincent must have written to him scores of times, but the newly discovered letter is the only one to have survived: the rest, as one of Tersteeg's sons revealed in an interview, were thrown into the stove and burned, along with hundreds of letters from other artists.

We find this incomprehensible now, but in those days most people kept in touch by writing letters, so anyone who participated in social life to any extent soon had hundreds, if not thousands, of sheets of paper to jettison. They can hardly be blamed for clearing out their desks once in a while. Van Gogh himself, who moved house often, did this of necessity. As a result,

most of the letters he received from Theo, his parents, Gauguin, Bernard, Van Rappard and others have been lost. That he in fact burned letters emerges from a short passage in a letter to Theo: 'The letter from Gauguin that I meant to send you, and thought for a moment to have burned with other papers, I have since found, and am enclosing.' In this case Gauguin's letter, which has survived, was unintentionally spared the flames.

It seems natural to think that Theo saved Vincent's letters for posterity because he realised how special they were, yet he also saved a great many letters from his parents, other members of the family, and friends and business contacts: some 2,000 of these have survived and are now part of the collection of the Van Gogh Museum. Sometimes they reveal important facts concerning Vincent that cannot be gleaned from his own letters.

Theo, however, was discerning enough to realise that the family letters would not make the most interesting reading for future generations, so he must have kept them out of love or respect for those who penned them. The

26
Portrait photograph of Wil van Gogh, c. 1887
Van Gogh Museum, Amsterdam

27
Portrait photograph of Jo van Gogh-Bonger and her son Vincent Willem, 1890
Van Gogh Museum, Amsterdam

Van Gogh children had, after all, been brought up with a strong sense of family values, and it was Theo, more than anyone, who had taken that education to heart. This, then, is the main reason for the preservation of so many of Vincent's letters.

All the same, Theo recognised that Vincent's letters were not just a run-of-the-mill correspondence. Around 1887-88, when Vincent was becoming known to a small circle, and critics had started to take an interest in him, Theo occasionally gave them some of Vincent's letters to read in an attempt to acquaint them with his exceptional artistic ideas, thus increasing their understanding of his unusual work.

## THE FRENCH LANGUAGE

The people in Paris interested in Van Gogh who were given Vincent's letters to read profited from the fact that since 1888 Vincent had been writing to Theo in French. This also gave Emile Bernard the possibility, after Van Gogh's death, to publish between 1893 and 1897 in the journal *Mercure de France* a series of instalments containing a wide selection of letter excerpts, an initiative that contributed greatly to the spread of Van Gogh's reputation.

Vincent had acquired French at an early age, since it was spoken by the Dutch upper classes, with whom he came into daily contact in his years at Goupil's in The Hague. Van Gogh had attended secondary school only briefly, but his employer no doubt required him to study French, and he acquired the habit of reading French literature in the original language. Moreover, he had been sent by the firm of Goupil to learn the art trade in Paris – where he stayed for several brief periods, amounting to a year altogether – and he had spent a long time in Belgium in the French-speaking environment of the Borinage. His stay in Paris in 1886-88 immersed him completely in the French language, while Theo had been living in Paris since 1879 and thus spoke French fluently. For someone like Van Gogh, with a great talent for languages and an eagerness to learn, it was only natural that French gained the upper hand.

It seems rather strange, if not downright puzzling, to think of two Dutch brothers corresponding with each other in French. The explanation was given by Van Gogh himself in a letter to his sister Wil: 'if you let me write in French, it makes my letter easier.' That French had supplanted his mother tongue is also noticeable in several letters written home in that same period – to his mother, for example – in which his Dutch is somewhat stiff and less fluent. In one of the last letters she received from her eldest son, his mother read, for instance: 'For me life might well remain solitary. I have not perceived those to whom I've been most attached other than through a glass, darkly. And yet there is a reason why there is sometimes more harmony in my work nowadays. Painting is something in itself. Last year I read somewhere that writing a book or making a painting was the same as having a child. I don't dare claim that for myself, though; I've always thought the latter was the most natural and best thing – only if it were so and if it were the same. That's why I sometimes do my utmost best, even though it's precisely *that* work that is the least understood, and it's the only tie that links the past and the present for me.' The clarity of his reasoning has suffered slightly here as a result of Van Gogh's diminished ability to express himself in his mother tongue.

## NOT A DIARY

Many people wonder whether Van Gogh's letters shed any light on his suicide or contain any signs that point to his tragic end. Strangely enough, his motives remain a secret, despite his many outpourings. Vincent did not write a farewell letter, and Theo could not possibly have sensed that things would turn out as they did when he received the letter in Paris that would prove to be the last, especially since it contained a couple of large letter sketches that, on the contrary, indicated a zest for work (28, 30-32). We do know, however, that Vincent had financial worries and was concerned about the future – both his own and that of Theo and his young family – because Theo was thinking of setting up as an independent art dealer, a potentially risky undertaking. From letters exchanged between Theo and his wife, Jo

43

Le jardin de Daubigny
avant plan d'herbe verte & rose
à gauche un buisson vert & lilas et une souche de plant
à feuillages blanchâtre. Au milieu un parterre
de roses. à droite une claie un mur et au dessus
du mur un noisetier à feuillage violet.

van Gogh-Bonger, we know that they found Vincent unduly anxious about it all, but this does not alter the fact that he experienced everything so intensely. Furthermore, he had little hope of recovering from his recurrent mental disturbances. All the same, his dramatic decision came like a bolt from the blue, and we will never be able to fathom his motives completely.

This should warn us not to view the letters as a kind of diary. We read, for example, that he met people and sometimes became friendly with them, but we learn nothing of the circumstances or the background to such acquaintances, except that he met Sien Hoornik in the street (which in this case says more than enough). He was a voracious reader, but we know little of how he acquired the hundreds of books mentioned in his letters, let alone the many hundreds more he must have read but never wrote about. He was constantly suffering from physical ailments, though we only read about them when they entailed great expense or prevented him from working. So we actually know relatively little about his daily life.

His letters were never intended to report events, certainly not in any detail. They were prompted primarily by the self-evident need for human contact and for exchanging ideas and feelings with a kindred spirit. To this end, it is only natural to talk about subjects that are not only close to one's heart but also arouse the interest – or at least the sympathy – of the other party. In the early years, the letters to Theo show that Vincent, who never had a bosom friend, needed his brother as a confidant and sounding-board. What bound them together was essentially their shared youth in the Brabant countryside and the family they came from, and of course art and literature.

When Vincent finally decided to become an artist, he was financially dependent on Theo, the generous patron, and his letters can then be read as an account of his artistic needs, choices and ideas. One would be going too far to describe the letters as business correspondence (as has sometimes been done), since the old, familiar themes persist. To be sure, receipt of his allowance often triggered a letter, but the content included far more than that, as evidenced by the quotations appearing throughout this book.

28
Last letter to Theo
Auvers-sur-Oise,
23 July 1890 (908/651)
Van Gogh Museum,
Amsterdam

29
Vincent van Gogh
*Daubigny's Garden*,
1890
Hiroshima Museum
of Art, Hiroshima

The relations between the brothers, however, especially during the first years of Vincent's artistic career, were no longer as unconstrained as they had once been.

The letters, then, were often prompted by strategic considerations. This is not to say that the obstinate moralist in Vincent always complied with his patron. He did not hesitate to make frequent attempts to win his brother over to his own, often unrealistic, view of things. Tension arose as soon as something that had always been taken for granted – what 'modern' art was,

30-32
Three sketches in the
last letter written by
Vincent to Theo
Auvers-sur-Oise,
23 July 1890 (908/651)
Van Gogh Museum,
Amsterdam

for instance, or what made art 'saleable' – was suddenly called into question. And as was only natural, Vincent – while writing – carefully selected what in his view was relevant and appropriate, leaving out facts that did not serve his purpose.

An example of this writing strategy is the oft-quoted lyrical passage about a journey that Van Gogh made through the countryside of Drenthe, hitching a ride with a farmer who was driving his horse and cart to the annual fair. Van Gogh described their arrival in a village along the way as follows: 'The ride into the village was really so beautiful. Huge mossy roofs on houses, barns, sheepfolds, sheds. The dwellings here are very wide, among oak trees of a superb bronze. Tones of golden green in the moss, of reddish or bluish or yellowish dark lilac greys in the soil, tones of inexpressible purity in the green of the little wheatfields, tones of black in the wet trunks, standing out against golden showers of whirling, swirling autumn leaves, which still hang in loose tufts, as if they were blown there, loosely and with the sky shining through them, on poplars, birches, limes, apple trees. The sky completely clear, luminous, not white but a lilac that cannot be deciphered, white in which one sees swirling red, blue, yellow, which reflects everything and one feels above one everywhere, which is vaporous and unites with the thin mist below, bringing everything together in a spectrum of delicate greys.'

It has sometimes been said that Van Gogh could have earned his living as a writer, an assertion that seems to be proved by this passage. In any case, it was not – or, at any rate, not only – the sheer passion of writing that produced this fine prose, nor was it the result of a spontaneous outburst of emotion. Vincent had conceived the absurd idea that Theo should abandon his excellent career to come and paint with him in Drenthe. Together they would have the strength to face the future, as other brothers had done: the painters Emile and Jules Breton, for example, and the writers Edmond and Jules de Goncourt. Vincent would teach Theo the trade; money was of secondary importance. The Drenthe landscape, he said, was just as beautiful as the Paris exhibition *One hundred masterpieces*, which Theo had apparently

described in such glowing terms – but drawing and painting in Drenthe was the more restful of the two (33). Vincent's written portrayal of the idyllic countryside was part of a month-long barrage of patronising advice, reproaches and fantasies about the future, which must have infuriated the generally patient and accommodating Theo. Even modern-day readers lose their patience now and then at such passages, and end up taking pity on poor Theo, who was sometimes given a good thrashing with the whip of brotherly love.

Thus the letters cannot possibly provide the basis for a detailed account of what Van Gogh actually *did* every day. They do, however, tell us how he *experienced* many of the important things in his life. In fact, Van Gogh's letters can be viewed as his most probing self-portrait.

## PAPER AND INK

When we speak of Van Gogh's letters we usually think of the volumes in which they have been published, but we can come closer to the story they tell by looking at the originals: more than 1,200 sheets of paper, most of them brittle and slightly yellowed, with tiny handwriting. Examining and reading the original letters close up gives one the sensation of peering over Van Gogh's shoulder and hearing the scratch of his quill pen – a feeling of witnessing, as it were, the intimate scene at the writing desk. The difference in time then seems to melt away, and history suddenly becomes tangible.

Unfortunately, the paper, which was fragile enough to begin with, is endangered by an unexpected foe: the ink with which the letters were written. Van Gogh normally used iron-gall ink, which contains a substance that corrodes paper. Precisely in the places where he used a lot of ink, such as in the sketches, serious damage has occurred, sometimes even causing the loss of text on the back of the sheet (34, 35). Global efforts are being made to develop a technique to halt such corrosion; the results are hopeful, but an effective remedy has yet to be found.

The facsimiles illustrated in this book show that Van Gogh's handwriting displayed both constants and variables. A comparison of letters written in the mid-1870s (36) with those of more than a decade later (37) reveals a hand that progresses from a somewhat stiff and immature appearance to a more personal and characteristic style – a development seen in most people's handwriting then and now. Its clarity suffered little in the process: once one has become accustomed to it, Van Gogh's writing is easily legible. He paid little heed, however, to the more general conventions of correspondence prevailing in his day. In the early years he wrote the place and date at the top of his letters, but the later ones lack

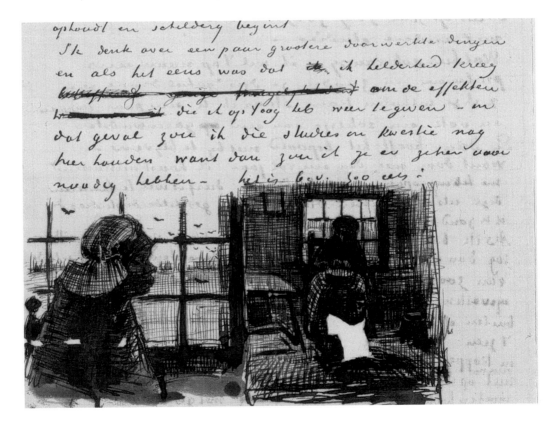

GOUPIL & Cᵉ

*Éditeurs Imprimeurs*

ESTAMPES FRANÇAISES & ÉTRANGÈRES

*Tableaux Modernes*

RUE CHAPTAL, 9, PARIS.

Succursales à la Haye, Londres, Berlin, New York.

*Paris, le* 24 Juli 1875

Waarde Theo,

Een paar dagen geleden kregen wij een schij van de Nittis, een gezicht in London op een regendag, Westminster bridge & the house of Parliament. Ik ging elken morgen & avond over Westminsterbridge & weet hoe dat er uit ziet als de zon achter Westminster abbey & the house of Parliament ondergaat & hoe het s'morgens vroeg is & s'winters met sneeuw & met mist. –

Toen ik dit schij zag voelde ik hoe ik van Londen houd.

Toch geloof ik het goed voor my is ik er van daan ben.. Dit in antwoord op uw vraag. Dat gij naar Londen gaat geloof ik zeker niet..

Dank voor 'Aus der Jugend zeit' & 'Um Mitternacht' van Rückert? 't Is werend schoon, 't laatst genoemde deed my denken aan 'La nuit de Décembre' van Musset. Ik wilde ik u dat kon zenden, doch heb het niet.

Gisteren hebben wy eene kist naar den Haag gezonden, waarin voor u wat ik u beloofde. Ik hoor Anna en Lies thuis zyn. ik zou hen wel eens willen zien. Heb het zoo goed mogelyk & schryf weer spoedig. En te serrant la main

Uw liefh broeder
Vincent

36
Letter to Theo
London, 24 July 1875
(29/32)
Van Gogh Museum, Amsterdam

37
Letter to John Peter Russell
Arles, c. 17 June 1888
(629/501a)
The Guggenheim Museum, New York
Thannhauser Collection

this information, beginning bluntly with such salutations as 'Cher Théo', 'Chère soeur' or 'Mon cher copain Bernard'. He often began immediately after this, on the same line, with what he had to say. One example is a letter to Bernard in which he started, directly after the salutation, by apologising for his poor handwriting (38). He was also adept at making use of the space available, writing in an extremely compact hand with the lines very close together. Only rarely was there any space left after his signature, and when there was, it was often filled up with a postscript. He did not hesitate to write afterthoughts in the margins, nor did he take pains to spell and punctuate correctly: the need for capitals was often ignored, and letters penned in an emotional state are occasionally made obvious by their unmistakably agitated hand, such as those written in a period of bitter clashes with his father (39).

52

I heard Rodin had a beautiful
head at the Salon.
I have been to the seaside for a
week and very likely am going thither
again soon. – That shore ~~~~~~
Sands – fine figures there
like Cimabue – straight stylish
Am working at a Sower: –

The great field all violet. The sky & sun very
yellow. It is a hard subject to treat.
Please remember me very kindly to
Mrs Russell – and in thought I heartily
shake hands. yours very truly
                                    Vincent

mon cher Bernard Pardonne moi si j'écris bien à la hâte je crains que ma lettre ne sera point lisible mais je veux te répondre tout de suite.

Sais-tu que nous avons été très bêtes Gauguin toi et moi de ne pas aller dans un même endroit. Mais lorsque Gauguin est parti moi j'étais pas encore sûr de pouvoir partir et lorsque toi tu es parti il y avait cet affreux argent du voyage et les mauvaises nouvelles que j'avais à donner des frais ici qui l'ont empêché. Si nous étions parti tous ensemble vers ici ce n'aurait pas été si bête car à trois nous eussions fait le ménage chez nous. Et maintenant que je suis un peu mieux orienté je commence à entrevoir des avantages ici.

Pour moi je me porte mieux ici que dans le nord - je travaille même en plein midi en plein soleil sans ombre aucune dans les champs de blé et voilà j'en jouis comme une cigale. Mon dieu si à 25 ans j'eusse connu ce pays au lieu d'y venir à 35 à cette époque j'étais enthousiasmé pour le gris ou l'encore plutôt l'absence de couleur. Je rêvais toujours de millet et puis j'avais des connaissances en hollande dans la catégorie de peintres mâtre ?

Voici croquis d'un
Semeur.
Grand terrain de mottes
de terre labourées
franchement violet en
grande partie.
Champs de blé mûr d'un
ton d'ocre jaune avec un
peu de carmin.
Le ciel jaune de chrome
presque aussi clair que
le soleil lui même qui
est jaune de chrome 1 avec
un peu de blanc tandis que
le reste du ciel est jaune
de chrome 1 et 2 mélangés
très jaune donc.
La blouse du semeur est bleu
et son pantalon blanc.
toile de 25 carrée

jaune
Jaune.
jaune ocre vieil or?
blanc
jaune

il y a bien des rappels de jaune dans le terrain des tons neutres résultantes du mélange du violet avec le jaune mais je me suis un peu foutu de la vérité de la couleur. J'aime des images naïves d'almanach plutôt - de vieil almanach de campagne où la grêle la neige la pluie le beau temps sont représentés d'une façon tout à fait primitive. ainsi qu'Anquetin avait si bien trouvé sa moisson. Je ne le cache pas que je ne déteste pas la campagne — y ayant été élevé des bouffées de souvenirs d'autrefois des aspirations vers cet infini dont le Semeur la gerbe sont les symboles m'enchantent encore comme autrefois

People act AS they FEEL. Our ACTIONS, our swift readiness or our hesitation, that's how we can be recognised – not by what we say with our lips – friendly or unfriendly. Good intentions, opinions, in fact that is less than nothing. You may think of me what you will, Theo, but I tell you it is not my imagination, I tell you, Pa is not willing.

I see now what I saw then, I spoke out four-square AGAINST Pa then, I speak now in any event, whatever may come of it, AGAINST Pa again, as being UNWILLING, as making it IMPOSSIBLE. It's damned sad, brother, the Rappards acted intelligently, but here!!!!!! And everything you did and do about it, 3/4 of it is rendered fruitless by them. It's wretched, brother. With a handshake.
Ever yours, Vincent.

38
Letter to Emile
Bernard
c. 19 June 1888
(630/B7)
The Morgan Library,
New York
Thaw Collection

39
Letter to Theo
Nuenen,
c. 7 December
1883 (412/345)
Van Gogh Museum,
Amsterdam

In certain letters there is a contrast between their idiosyncratic and unconventional finish and the great care Van Gogh lavished on them: he clearly reread them to make improvements both to the content, by inserting words or sentences, and to the handwriting, by going over letters to make them more legible. Van Gogh seldom made a rough copy; he usually wrote whatever came out of his pen, as he put it. Some letters of which we have another version, finished or not, suggest painstaking preparation. Nevertheless, it seems more likely that these are outdated versions or rejected attempts that he discarded, which were obsolete when the time came to finish and send them.

Rejected texts of a completely different kind are the passages that Van Gogh crossed out. The printed copy does not reveal the handwritten version that preceded the final text; by examining the original letters, one can sometimes decipher interesting or enlightening words or passages that reveal that the crossed-out text was not completely innocent. Sometimes these deletions were the result of Van Gogh's strategic approach to letter-writing, while at other times they involved passages that strangers were not supposed to see. An example of the latter is a small sheet with a sketch of his painting *Starry night above the Rhône* (40, 42). The back contains part of a letter, but the lines have been emphatically crossed out (41). They are addressed to Paul Gauguin and refer to a difference of opinion between Gauguin and Theo on the one hand and Vincent on the other, concerning lowering the prices of certain paintings. After Van Gogh had written this, however, he decided to send the little sketch to his friend Eugène Boch (44), who of course had nothing to do with this personal matter.

Some sheets display obvious differences in the ductus – that is to say, the way the pen is wielded, creating the characteristic rhythm and slope of the handwriting – although the writing remains recognisable as the work of one hand (43). This suggests that Van Gogh put the letter aside and resumed writing later on. We know that he sometimes composed a letter in stages, during breaks from drawing or painting; moreover, a change in ductus can simply be the result of a pause for thought. In a couple of cases we

40
Sketch enclosed
in a letter to
Eugène Boch
Arles, 2 October 1888
Van Gogh Museum,
Amsterdam

41
Verso of fig. 40

42
Vincent van Gogh,
*Starry night above
the Rhône*, 1888
Musée d'Orsay, Paris

Ces derniers jours vent & pluie j'ai
travaillé chez moi à l'étude dont j'ai fait
un croquis dans la lettre de Bernard
Je voulais arriver a y mettre des couleurs
comme dans les vitraux et un dessin
à lignes fermes.
Suis en train de lire Pierre et Jean de Guy
de Maupassant. c'est beau - as tu lu
la préface expliquant la liberté qu'a l'artiste
d'exagérer de créer une nature plus belle
plus simple plus consolante dans un roman
puis expliquant ce que voulait peut être bien
dire le mot de Flaubert le talent est une
~~bonne~~ longue patience - et l'originalité
~~étant~~ un effort de volonté et d'observation
intense.
Il y a ici un portique gothique
que je commence a trouver
admirable le portique de St Trophime
mais c'est si cruel si monstrueux comme
un cauchemar chinois que même ce beau
monument d'un si grand style me semble d'un
autre monde auquel je suis aussi bien
aise de ne pas apartenir que le monde
glorieux du Romain Néron —
Faut-il dire la vérité et y ajouter que
les zouaves les bordels les adorables petites
arlésiennes qui s'en vont faire leur première
communion le prêtre en surplis qui ressemble
a un rinoceros dangereux les buveurs d'absinthe
me paraissent aussi des êtres d'un autre monde

43
Letter to Theo
Arles, 21 or 22 March
1888 (589/470)
Van Gogh Museum,
Amsterdam

44
Vincent van Gogh,
*Portrait of Eugène Boch*
(*'Le poète'*), 1888
Musée d'Orsay, Paris

may safely assume that dim lamplight and too much drink combined to produce such erratic handwriting.

## LETTER SKETCHES
An attractive feature of Van Gogh's letters, and one that adds immensely to
their art-historical value, is their frequent embellishment with a small drawing or the inclusion of a loose-leaf sketch, which he referred to as 'krabbelt-
jes' (little scratches) or 'croquis' (sketches). Van Gogh, incidentally, was not

verdâtres – Car malgré l'inscription les personnes ont l'air triste
en contradiction avec le titre. Sur ce
ciré il y a des reflets que donne la
sur les parties bosses qui donne
richesse –
Je vais l'envoyer à Paris dans quel
Peut être celui plaira plus que ceux
de Haan vous dit bien des choses
Cordialement à vous
                    P. Gauguin
P.S. Je sais que vous fatigues quand v
aussi je ne demande pas de lettre (mais
le plaisir que j'ai à vous lire
        Le service militaire de Bernard
remis à un an pour (Santé) –

au Pouldu près Quimper (finistère)

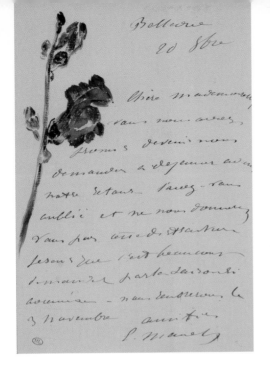

the only one to do this. Many writers and artists have made – and continue to make – drawings in letters, to the extent that this activity can be considered an epistolary sub-genre. There are detailed and colourful letter sketches by the hand of Paul Signac, Stéphane Mallarmé, Paul Verlaine, Henri de Toulouse-Lautrec and Paul Gauguin (45), to name but a few of Van Gogh's contemporaries. Letter sketches existed in all shapes and sizes, and they served a wide variety of purposes.

Van Gogh was rarely interested in illustrating a letter merely for the fun of it. He was not light-hearted enough for that, and he had no need to be charming – something that gave rise, for example, to the great number of beautiful drawings in the letters of Edouard Manet (46). For Van Gogh the sketches had but one goal: to make clear to Theo or other correspondents what a particular painting looked like, either a finished one or a work in progress. At the beginning of his artistic career, he also needed to prove to Theo that he was progressing. In Etten he once wrote a letter containing twelve sketches, some of them in colour (48). They were intended to convince Theo of his commitment and to show him his depictions of the peasants and labourers he idolised.

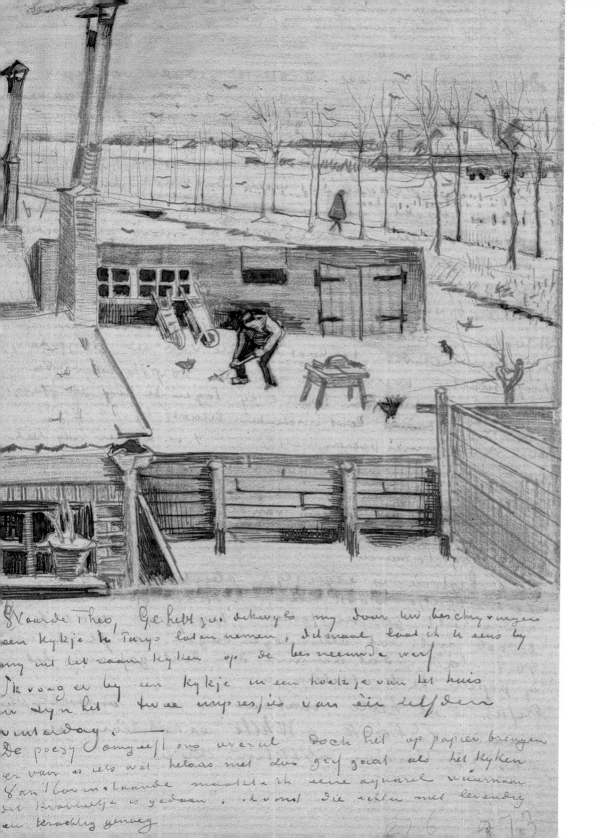

Waarde Theo, Ge hebt zoo dikwyls my door uw beschryvingen
een kykje te Parijs laten nemen, ditmaal laat ik u eens by
my uit het raam kyken op de besneeuwde werf
Ik voeg er by een kykje in een hoekje van het huis
in zyn het twee impressies van éen zelfden
winterdag.
De poesy omgeeft ons overal doch het op papier brengen
er van is iets wat helaas niet zoo gaat als het kyken.
Van 't bovenstaande maakte ik eene aquarel waarnaar
dit krabbeltje is gedaan, komt die echter met levendig
en krachtig genoeg

47
Letter to Theo
The Hague,
21-28 March 1883
(330-R330)
Van Gogh Museum,
Amsterdam

48
Letter to Theo
Etten, mid-September
1881 (171/150)
Van Gogh Museum,
Amsterdam

The value of the sketches lies in the fact that they forced Van Gogh to convey the essence of a drawing or painting. Usually drawn with ordinary writing ink, they were sometimes supplied with colour indications, which we can compare with the painting, as in the case of the enchanting *Blossoming pear tree* (49, 50). A couple of the sketches even supplement his known oeuvre, because they represent an earlier version of an existing work

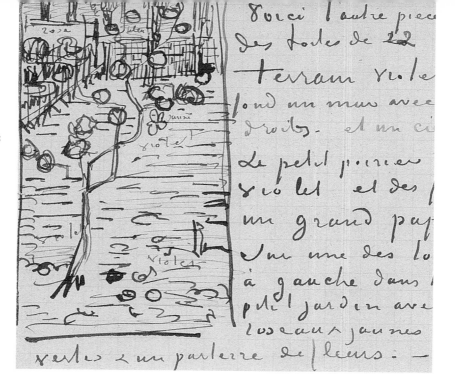

or the only image of a lost work. In the letter to Eugène Boch mentioned above, for example, there is a sketch Van Gogh made after an unknown painting of the park in front of the Yellow House (51).

The letter sketches display a clear development in style, which derives directly from the astonishingly fast development of Van Gogh's 'draughtsman's fist', as he himself called it. The early sketches are rather dark and densely worked, whereas the later ones are much lighter and airier. Although sometimes quite small, they steadily gain in diversity of expressive means and look less heavy than those dating from the first years. Gradually Van Gogh became so sure of his draughtsmanship that he occasionally used the letter sketches – and rightly so – to show what he was capable of, as in the letter to Emile Bernard in which he recounts an excursion to Les Saintes-Maries-de-la-Mer on the Mediterranean coast (52, 53).

Finally, there are a couple of dozen sketches that are very useful for understanding Van Gogh's working methods. The drawn view of his studio, for example, shows us how he experimented with the angle of light, using shutters he had made specially for this purpose (55). No less instructive is

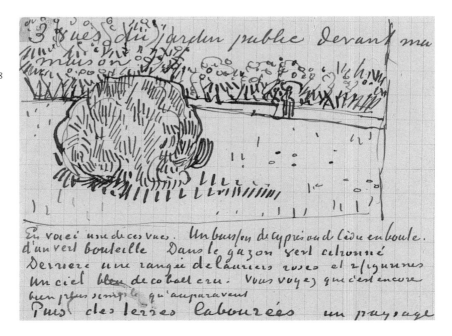

his explanation of the perspective frame he had made to help him in the
correct rendering of depth and proportions (54); indeed, his drawings and
paintings frequently bear traces of its application. One of the most important tools of the painter, his palette, was also illustrated for Theo (56), as
were the brushes Vincent asked him to order (57).

## LETTERS AND ART

The richness of the letters should not make us lose sight of the fact that Van
Gogh's stature is primarily due to his fundamental importance for the art
of modern times. It is therefore vital to ask what the letters contribute to
our understanding of Van Gogh's drawings and paintings.

The answer is: everything. In every phase of his career as an artist –
except, alas, the years in Paris – the letters treat in detail, from both the personal and the artistic viewpoint, Van Gogh's ambitions and the difficulties
he encountered. Had he been educated at an academy, our knowledge of
the training painters generally received in the nineteenth century would

Wel hoop ik nog dezen zomer een jaar
my te oefenen met houtskool voor
grootere schetsen met het oog om later
te schilderen en wat ruimer formaat. —
En 't is daarvoor dat ik weer een nieuw en
hoop ik beter perspectiefraam laat maken
dat in ongelijken duingrond b.v. lekker vast
staat met twee stijlen

b.v. op deze manier
Dat wat we zamen op Scheveningen zagen.
Zand — Zee — lucht — is iets dat
ik zeer zeker van mijn leven wel eens hoop
it te drukken.
Natuurlijk heb ik niet alles wat gy my
gegeven hebt n eens uitgegeven — ofschoon
it moet it wel zeggen de pyzer van een ander
my weer geducht tegenvielen — en er als men nagaat

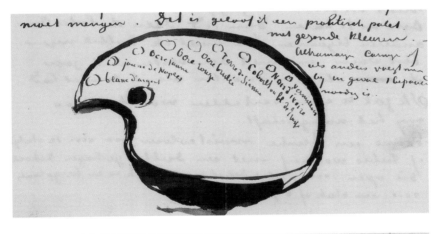

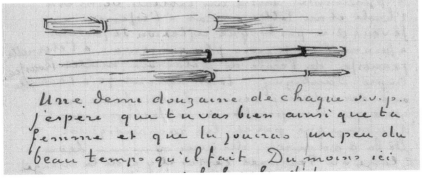

already give us some idea of the traditions informing his art and the skills he would have been taught. However, Van Gogh was self-taught, and unorthodox at that. In 1885, when visiting the important museums in Amsterdam, including the recently opened Rijksmuseum, he looked for the first time with an artist's eye at such great painters as Frans Hals and Rembrandt, and made the liberating discovery that they, too, often used very loose brushstrokes. 'Let people prattle on about technique as they will, with hollow, hypocritical, Pharisee words – the true painters allow themselves to be guided by that conscience that is called sentiment; their soul, their brains aren't led by the brush, but the brush is led by their brains. Moreover, it's the canvas that's afraid of a true painter, and not the painter who's afraid of the canvas.' He derided 'custom', 'tradition' and 'practice', seeking in his own way a suitable working method and the means to achieve what he envisioned on paper or canvas.

This does not mean that the finished result always shows how a certain work of art came about or what Van Gogh had hoped to express, so we are fortunate to have the letters, which provide important information about his technique and supply clues to the interpretation of his work. Of course, in his correspondence he commented on only some of the more than 2,000 works of art we know by his hand, but his comments afford a foothold for closer study of those works. They show clearly that Van Gogh, from the beginning to the end of his artistic career, sought to imbue his work with a message. As a budding artist he wrote, 'I want to do things that *touch* people'; in 1889 he described what he was striving to produce: 'consolatory art for distressed hearts'. He aimed at moving the viewer while demonstrating something essential about human existence, offering consolation for the inadequacies of life. In the Dutch years he did this in the tradition of Millet and Jozef Israëls, by rendering an image that betrays a certain sentiment – a literary approach, as he said himself. With regard to what he intended to portray in The potato eaters (22), he wrote: 'I really have wanted to make it so that people get the idea that these folk, who are eating their potatoes by the light of their little lamp, have tilled the earth themselves with these hands they are putting in the dish, and so it speaks of MANUAL LABOUR and – that they have thus honestly *earned* their food. I wanted it to give the idea of a wholly different way of life from ours – civilised people.'

After his artistic transformation in Paris, he understood that he could express something not only with the image depicted, with the anecdotal element of the picture, but also with the pictorial *means*, such as colour and brushwork. How he thought this worked is revealed in a letter in which he describes the underlying idea behind *The bedroom* (59) (with which he sought to express 'an absolute calm') and *The night café* (60). Writing about the latter painting to Theo, Vincent said: 'In my picture of the Night Café I have tried to express that the café is a place where one can ruin oneself, go mad, commit a crime. Well, I sought – through contrasts of soft pink and blood

58
Sketch enclosed
in a letter to Theo
Arles, 16 October
1888 (710/554)
Van Gogh Museum,
Amsterdam

59
Vincent van Gogh,
*The bedroom*, 1888
Van Gogh Museum,
Amsterdam

Vincent van Gogh,
*The night café*, 1888
Yale University Art
Gallery, New Haven

red and the colour of wine, of soft Louis XV green and Veronese green contrasting with the yellow-greens and the hard blue-greens, all of this in an
atmosphere of infernal fire of pale sulphur – to express the powerful dark-
nesses of a dram shop.'

We are also particularly indebted to the letters for clarifying the handful of Arles paintings that seem so out of place in his work because of the
flat and schematic impression that they make, such as *Garden at Etten* (5)
and *Woman reading a novel* (61). The explanation is that he had let himself be
challenged by Gauguin into working from memory instead of from life,
using his imagination instead of working from nature.

## VAN GOGH'S FAME

Would Van Gogh have become as famous as he is if we did not have those splendid letters that elucidate his exceptional life and the world behind his works? That question is both provocative and complex. We cannot turn back the clock, but we may assume that without the letters his fame would have taken on a different character. Even so, we can confirm that the dissemination of Van Gogh's work and his letters have more or less kept pace with one another, making them nearly inseparable from the historical viewpoint. Just as his letters and his work are bound together in our minds, likewise our appreciation of him tends to combine the man and the artist. This was never his intention, for he hoped to speak through his drawings and paintings alone.

Furthermore, it was never Van Gogh's aim to have his letters published, though some would have us believe otherwise. He did in fact save Bernard's letters, about which he wrote to Theo in September 1888: 'they are sometimes really interesting, you will read them some day, there is already quite a stack.' He also advised his brother to save letters from artists, referring to artists' letters in the true sense of the word, that is to say, an exchange of artistic ideas. It is possible that to some extent he saw his own correspondence with Gauguin and Bernard in this light, and he knew that his friends sometimes let each other read his letters. He was, moreover, an avid reader of biographies and artists' autobiographical writing, then an up-and-coming genre. For his part, however, Van Gogh never aspired to publish his letters and always shunned public attention – even when it was directed towards his paintings.

Does this mean that we are being indiscreet if we nose around in Van Gogh's private correspondence, if we publish it in dozens of languages for a global market consisting of hundreds of thousands of readers? In one sense: yes. His letters were not intended for us – only for Theo, a few other members of the family and some friends. His sister Lies was not happy when, in 1914, her sister-in-law Jo van Gogh-Bonger presented the world with the letters Vincent had written to Theo. Over the years, however, Van

61
Vincent van Gogh,
*Woman reading a novel*,
1888
Private collection

62
Sketch in a letter
to Wil van Gogh
Arles, c. 12 November
1888 (725/W9)
Van Gogh Museum,
Amsterdam

Gogh has grown into a larger-than-life personality. Though he thought he would play no more than a secondary role in the future of art, for more than a hundred years now he has been an icon, a role model – and not only for artists. The idealism and determination permeating his letters are an inspiration to every reader. He is to many of us what his own heroes – Rembrandt, Millet and Delacroix – were to him. Indeed, this knowledge might have reconciled him to the fact that his letters, and not just his art, are now known throughout the world.

Daar er weder een brief naar U toegaat zoo sluit ik een woordje.
Van harte hoop ik dat gij het goed maakt. 'k Eens een half uurtje
Zult kunnen vinden om my weer eens te schrijven.

Ik wil U nu nog zeggen wat ik heb uitgevoerd sedert ik U het laatst
geschreven heb.
Vooreerst twee groote teekeningen (krijt els of wat sepia) &
Knotwilgen zoo ongeveer als onderstaand schetsje.

Verder een dito maar in de hoogte van de Leursche we..
Dan heb ik weer een paar keer model gehad spitter en
mandemaker.
En dan heb ik van oom Cent verl.week een verfdoos gek..
die vrij goed is zeker goed genoeg om mee te beginnen
(de verf is van Paillard). En daar ben ik zeer blij mede

Nu heb ik dadelijk eens beproefd een soort aquarel te
maken als bovenstaand motief.

# THE LETTERS OF VAN GOGH: A FEW STATISTICS

Total number of extant letters: c. 900
  In Dutch: c. 585
  In French: c. 310
  In English: c. 6
Letters written by Van Gogh: c. 820
Letters written to Van Gogh: c. 80

Present whereabouts:
Van Gogh Museum, Amsterdam: c. 845
The Morgan Library, New York: 20
Other museums and public archives: 10
Private collections: c. 25

Characteristics:
Number of sheets: c. 1200
Number of pages: c. 3800 (an average of
4.2 pages per letter)
Shortest letter: 1 page
Longest letter: 16 pages
Usual length: 1 sheet comprising 4 pages
(390 letters)
Letters containing sketches: 140
Total number of sketches: 220

Number of extant letters written by
Vincent van Gogh to:
• Theo: c. 650
• Anthon van Rappard: 58
• Emile Bernard: 22
• Paul Gauguin: 16
• Wil van Gogh: 23

The other surviving letters by Van Gogh
are addressed to:
• Charles Angrand, a French painter
  Van Gogh met in Paris
• Albert Aurier, art critic
• Eugène Boch, a Belgian painter Van Gogh
  met in Arles
• Egbert Borchers, an acquaintance from
  The Hague
• H.J. Furnée, seller of artists' requisites in
  The Hague
• P. Furnée, surveyor (son of H.J. Furnée),
  pupil of Van Gogh
• M. and Mme Ginoux, proprietors of the
  Café de la Gare in Arles
• The Van Gogh family: parents, his sister
  Anna, his Uncle Cor
• Caroline (& Willem van Stockum-)
  Haanebeek, acquaintances from The Hague
• J. van Hombergh, mayor of Nuenen
• J.J. Isaacson, Dutch art critic and
  correspondent in Paris
• Anton Kerssemakers, acquaintance from
  Eindhoven, pupil of Van Gogh
• A.H. Koning, Dutch art critic and
  an acquaintance of Theo
• Horace Mann Livens, English painter,
  with whom Van Gogh associated in Antwerp
• John Peter Russell, an Australian artist
  Van Gogh met in Paris
• Paul Signac, French painter
• H.G. Tersteeg (& family), Van Gogh's boss
  at Goupil's in The Hague
• M.A. de Zwart, Van Gogh's landlord in
  The Hague

63
Letter to Theo
Etten, c. 12 October
1881
(173/151)
Van Gogh Museum,
Amsterdam

81

My dear Rappard,

Letter to Anthon
van Rappard
Etten, 12 October 1881
(172/R1)
Van Gogh Museum,
Amsterdam

I just received 'Gavarni, l'homme & l'oeuvre', accept my thanks for returning it. In my opinion, Gavarni is a very great artist, and certainly very interesting as a human being as well. Without doubt, at times he did things that weren't good, his behaviour towards Thackeray & Dickens, to name but a few, but there are such things in all characters.

And he, too, seems to have regretted it, because later he sent drawings to those people whom he had once treated with insufficient cordiality. And Thackeray himself adopted a similar attitude towards Balzac, and went even further I believe, but that doesn't alter the fact that at bottom those men were kindred spirits, even though this was not always clear to them.

When I received the book this morning, I thought 'now he certainly won't come himself, otherwise he would have kept it until he came'. I don't need to assure you once more that all of us here would very much like to see you again, and hope so much that, even if you don't come for long, you won't stay away entirely.

I'm very eager to hear about your plans for the winter. Supposing you go to Antwerp, Brussels or Paris, be sure to come and visit us on your way, and if you stay in Holland then I won't give up hope either; it's also beautiful here in the winter, and we surely could do something, if not outdoors then working from a model in the house of some peasant or other.

I've been drawing a lot from the model lately, since I've found a couple of models who are willing enough. And I have all kinds of studies of diggers, sowers &c., men & women. I'm working a lot with charcoal & Conté at the moment, & have also tried sepia & watercolour. Anyway, I can't say whether you'd see improvement in my drawings, but most certainly a change.

I hope to visit Mauve again soon to discuss the question of whether or not I should start painting. If I start, I shall also persevere. I'll talk it over again with various people before I begin, though. I realize more and more as time goes on that it was good that I set my mind more specifically on figure drawing. Indirectly, this really does influence landscape drawing as well, because one learns to concentrate.

I'd send you a couple of sketches if I had the time, but I'm very occupied with all kinds of things, though later you'll receive some more. Should you not stay in the country, I would be pleased to have your address. In any case, I'll have more to write to you this winter. Do you mind if I keep Karl Robert, Le fusain, for a while longer? It's because, working with charcoal now, I still need it so much, but if I go to The Hague I'll see to it that I get one myself. It would surprise me very much if I weren't to stay in Etten this winter – this is my plan at least, anyway not to go abroad. Because I've been rather fortunate since coming back here to Holland, not only in drawing but in other things as well. Anyway, I'll carry on here for a while, I spent so many years abroad, in England as well as in France & Belgium, that it's high time I stayed here for a while. You know what's absolutely beautiful these days, the road to the station & to De Leur with the old pollard willows, you have a sepia of it yourself. I can't tell you how beautiful those trees are now. Made around 7 large studies of several of the trunks.

I'm absolutely certain that if you were here now when the leaves are falling, even if only for a week, you would make something beautiful of it. If you feel like coming, it would give all of us here pleasure.

Accept my parents' warm regards and a handshake in thought from me, & believe me

Ever yours,
Vincent

My dear Theo,

Letter to Theo
Drenthe,
c. 5 November 1883
(405/339a)
Van Gogh Museum,
Amsterdam

What I think is the best life, oh without even the slightest shadow of a doubt, is a life made up of long years of being in touch with nature out of doors – and with the something on high – unfathomable, 'awfully Unnameable', because one cannot find a name for it – above that nature. Be a peasant – be, if that were fitting at the present time, a village clergyman or schoolmaster – be, and given the present time that is the form that seems to me to be the most fitting, be a Painter – and in so doing as a person you will, after that spell of years of outdoor life and manual work, as a person you will, in the end and in the passage of years, gradually become something better & deeper. I firmly believe this. In my view, the way one starts out, cleverer, not so clever, with more or with fewer privileges of favourable circumstances, is far from being the most important thing. If one starts on it one must only do it with the belief in the need to be in touch with nature, with the belief that if one takes that path one cannot go wrong, and walks straightest. And – added to that is just precisely that if one had things easy, a sort of living on private means, it would be of very little help, for it is precisely many a hard day, precisely many forlorn attempts, that make someone better.

And what I believe does a great deal of good is if one doesn't work absolutely alone, because the work inevitably absorbs one, but one doesn't become lost in that absorption because each advises the other, can keep the other on the right path.

If you were to talk to people, they would say to you, what are you thinking of, what a reckless gamble to give up this & that, etc. In short, people would think it crazy – think it a mistake. For myself, I would think the recklessness must lie in a different outlook on life from the one I'm talking about – that of Painter – I think reckless is precisely binding oneself irrevocably to the city & city affairs.

People will tell you, you're a fanatic and you don't foresee the future – in my view you do foresee the future, in my view in a period like the one you are in now, certainly after such emotional experiences as you have had, one cannot be fanatical then, one is in a period of disenchantment. People needn't try to twist things with me, that won't wash with me. I feel my own incurable melancholy about the way one thing & another has gone, and they try to tell me I was in a mood of 'rash, youthful fanaticism'. Far, very far from it. In your frame of mind one is in damned earnest.

It isn't something soft, something sweet that you think you will find; no, you know that it will be a fight as if with a rock; no, you know that nature cannot be conquered or made submissive without a terrible fight, without more than the ordinary level of patience.

And people would imagine your state of mind, if one were to talk about becoming a painter, as a delusion of a bed of roses.

I ask you, what do people who might only vaguely begin to think that way know about it? That's the way the world is, though, but that is only one of its enormities when it comes to misunderstanding, by no means the worst. It is precisely because of this deadly contrariness of public opinion that it's obvious that one should ignore it. One feels that things are wretched and all too wrong; – however calm and cheerful and full of serenity by nature, one becomes utterly melancholy, feels that this cannot be different, and then, what is more practical than to say, if I don't do something about it I will lose my energy and vitality, I'm going to refresh, renew myself in nature, I'm just going to tackle it very differently, and I'll arrange it in such a way that in a few years' time, say, I have altogether new, firm ground beneath my feet.

I have no patience with the 'so-called' common sense (fake article, inexpressibly different from the real thing) that one is supposed to use, that one is said not to use if one departs from the ordinary or takes a risk. I say, I have no patience with it. For me, it is precisely because my natural common sense, if I use it to reflect, leads me to such very different results from the narrow-minded worldly wisdom & cautious, half-hearted sincerity of some people, that I have no patience with it.

Oh that procrastination, oh those hesitations, oh that failure to believe that good is good, that black is black and white is white. Dear brother – I cannot speak; now, at this moment, I am glad that I can only express myself falteringly, chaotically and roughly. I am glad that I cannot write to you coherently like Tersteeg and Pa – at this moment.

I believe so strongly in your artistic ability that to me you will be an artist as soon as you pick up a brush or a piece of chalk and, clumsily or not clumsily, make something.

Before you can express yourself in your work, namely a straightforward, thinking manly soul – peaceable – good – before you can do that, a very great deal has to happen, but it will come. At first one does not paint as one is, certainly not when one is good. But right away there is a je ne sais quoi – I already see it now in your word pictures of bits of Paris &c., I would see it in your first sketches or studies too.

When I think of Pa himself, then it seems to me that it is to his contact with nature that Pa owes his goodness, and his mistake, to my mind, is to attach more value to other things than they are basically worth. To me, Pa is someone who did not have any knowledge of the intimate lives of some great men when he should have had it. I mean that, in my view, Pa does not know, did not know nor ever will know what the soul of modern civilization is. What is it? The eternal, the very greatest simplicity and truth – Dupré, Daubigny, Corot, Millet, Israëls, Herkomer – not to mention Michelet, Hugo, Zola, Balzac, a host more from the more distant & more recent past. If prejudices, which Pa has carried with him throughout his life with an assiduousness worthy of a better cause, stand in his way – to me he is a black ray. The only criticism I have of Pa is: why isn't he a white ray? This is harsh criticism, so be it, I can't help it. To you I say, look for white ray, white, do you hear! With a handshake.

Ever yours,
Vincent


I don't say, far, very far be it for me to say that I have a white ray, but I am not embarrassed to say it exists, that white light – and I seek it, that alone do I consider simple.

My dear old Bernard,

A thousand thanks for sending your drawings; I very much like the avenue of plane trees beside the sea, with two women chatting in the foreground and the promenaders. Also

the woman under the apple tree

the woman with the umbrella

then the four drawings of nude women, especially the one washing herself, a grey effect embellished with black, white, yellow, brown. It's charming.

Ah... Rembrandt.... all admiration for baudelaire apart – i venture to assume, especially on the basis of those verses.... that he knew more or less nothing about rembrandt. I have just found and bought here a little etching after rembrandt, a study of a nude man, realistic and simple; he's standing, leaning against a door or column in a dark interior. A ray of light from above skims his down-turned face and the bushy red hair.

You'd think it a Degas for the body, true and felt in its animality.

But see, have you ever looked closely at 'the ox' or the interior of a butcher's shop in the Louvre? You haven't looked closely at them, and Baudelaire infinitely less so.

It would be a treat for me to spend a morning with you in the Dutch gallery. All that is barely describable. But in front of the paintings I could show you marvels and miracles that are the reason why, for me, the primitives really don't have my admiration first and foremost and most directly.

But there you are; I'm so far from eccentric. A Greek statue, a peasant by Millet, a Dutch portrait, a nude woman by Courbet or Degas, these calm and modelled perfections are the reason why many other things, the primitives as well as the Japanese, seem to me.... like WRITING WITH A PEN; they interest me infinitely.. but something complete, a perfection, makes the infinite tangible to us.

And to enjoy such a thing is like coitus, the moment of the infinite.

For instance, do you know a painter called Vermeer, who, for example, painted a very beautiful Dutch lady, pregnant? This strange painter's palette is blue, lemon yellow, pearl grey, black, white. Of course, in his few paintings there are, if it comes to it, all the riches of a complete palette, but the arrangement of lemon yellow, pale

Letter to Emile
Bernard
Arles, 29 July 1888
(651/B12)
Van Gogh Museum,
Amsterdam

blue, pearl grey is as characteristic of him as the black, white, grey, pink is of Velázquez.

Anyway, I know, Rembrandt and the Dutch are scattered around museums and collections, and it's not very easy to form an idea of them if you only know the Louvre.

However, it's Frenchmen, C. Blanc, Thoré, Fromentin, certain others, who have written better than the Dutch on that art.

Those Dutchmen had scarcely any imagination or fantasy, but great taste and the art of arrangement; they did not paint Jesus Christs, the Good Lord and others. Rembrandt though – indeed, but he's the only one (and there are relatively few biblical subjects in his oeuvre), he's the only one who, as an exception, did Christs, &c.

And in his case, they hardly resemble anything by other religious painters; it's a metaphysical magic.

So, Rembrandt painted angels – he makes a portrait of himself as an old man, toothless, wrinkled, wearing a cotton cap – first, painting from life in a mirror – he dreams, dreams, and his brush begins his own portrait again, but from memory, and its expression becomes sadder and more saddening; he dreams, dreams on, and why or how I do not know, but just as Socrates and Mohammed had a familiar genie, Rembrandt, behind this old man who bears a resemblance to himself, paints a supernatural angel with a Da Vinci smile.

I'm showing you a painter who dreams and who paints from the imagination, and I started off by claiming that the character of the Dutch is that they invent nothing, that they have neither imagination nor fantasy.

Am I illogical? No. Rembrandt invented nothing, and that angel and that strange Christ; it's – that he knew them, felt them there.

Delacroix paints a Christ through the unexpectedness of a light lemon note, this colourful and luminous note in the painting being what the ineffable strangeness and charm of a star is in a corner of the firmament.

Rembrandt works with values in the same way as Delacroix with colours.

Now, there's a gulf between the method of Delacroix and Rembrandt and that of all the rest of religious painting.

I'll write to you again soon. This to thank you for your drawings, which give me enormous pleasure.

Have just finished portrait of young girl of 12, brown eyes, black hair and eyebrows, flesh yellow grey, the background white, strongly tinged with veronese, jacket blood-red with violet stripes, skirt blue with large orange spots, an oleander flower in her sweet little hand.

I'm so worn out from it that I hardly have a head for writing. So long, and again, many thanks.

Ever yours,
Vincent

Letter to Wil
van Gogh
Arles,
c. 9-14 September
1888 (681/w7)
Van Gogh Museum,
Amsterdam

Your letter gave me great pleasure, and today I have the leisure to reply to you in peace and quiet. So your visit to Paris was a great success. I would really like it if you were to come here too next year. At the moment I'm furnishing the studio in such a way as always to be able to put someone up. Because there are 2 small rooms upstairs, which look out on a very pretty public garden, and where you can see the sunrise in the morning. I shall arrange one of these rooms for putting up a friend, and the other one will be for me.

I want nothing there but straw-bottomed chairs and a table and a deal bed. The walls whitewashed, the tiles red. But in it I want a great wealth of portraits and painted studies of figures, which I plan to do as I go along. I have one to start with, the portrait of a young Belgian Impressionist; I've painted him as something of a poet, his refined & nervous head standing out against a deep ultramarine background of the night sky, with the twinkling of the stars.

Now the other room, I would like it almost elegant, with a walnut bed with a blue blanket.

And all the rest, the dressing-table and the chest of drawers too, in matt walnut. I want to stuff at least 6 very large canvases in this tiny little room, the way the Japanese do, especially the huge bouquets of sunflowers. You know that the Japanese instinctively look for contrasts, and eat sweetened peppers, salty sweets, and fried ices and frozen fried dishes. So, too, following the same system you should probably only put very small paintings in a large room, but in a very small room you'll put a lot of big ones.

I hope the day will come when I'll be able to show you this beautiful part of the world.

I have just finished a canvas of a café interior at night, lit by lamps. Some poor night-prowlers are sleeping in a corner. The room is painted red, and inside, in the gaslight, the green billiard-table, which casts an immense shadow over the floor. In this canvas there are 6 or 7 different reds, from blood-red to delicate pink, contrasting with the same number of pale or dark greens.

Today I sent Theo a drawing of it, which is like a Japanese print.

Theo wrote telling me that he has given you some Japanese prints. It's certainly the most practical way of getting to understand the direction that painting has taken at present. Colourful and bright.

For myself, I don't need Japanese prints here, because I'm always saying to myself that I'm in Japan here. That as a result I only have to open my eyes and paint right in front of me what makes an impression on me.

Have you seen a tiny little mask of a fat, smiling Japanese woman at our place? The expression on that little mask is really surprising.

Did you think of taking one of my paintings with you for yourself? I hope so, and I'm quite intrigued to know which you would have chosen. I myself thought you would have taken the white huts under the blue sky among the greenery, which I did at Saintes-Maries, on the Mediterranean.

I should have gone back to Saintes-Maries already, now that there are people on the beach. But anyway, I have so much to do right here.

I definitely want to paint a starry sky now. It often seems to me that the night is even more richly coloured than the day, coloured in the most intense violets, blues and greens.

If you look carefully you'll see that some stars are lemonish, others have a pink, green, forget-me-not blue glow. And without labouring the point, it's clear that to paint a starry sky it's not nearly enough to put white spots on blue-black.

My house here is painted outside in the yellow of fresh butter, with garish green shutters, and it's in the full sun on the square, where there's a green garden of plane trees, oleanders, acacias. And inside, it's all whitewashed, and the floor's of red bricks. And the intense blue sky above. Inside, I can live and breathe, and think and paint. And it seems to me that I should go further into the south rather than going back up north, because I have too great a need of the strong heat so that my blood circulates normally. I'm in really much better health here than in Paris.

Now I have scarcely a doubt that for you, too, you would like the south enormously. It's the sun, that has never sufficiently penetrated us northerners.

I started this letter several days ago, up to here, and I'm picking it up again now. I was interrupted precisely by the work that a new painting of the outside of a café in the evening has been giving me these past few days. On the terrace, there are little figures of people drinking. A huge yellow lantern lights the terrace, the façade, the pavement, and even projects light over the cobblestones of the street, which takes on a violet-pink tinge. The gables of the houses on a street that leads away under the blue sky studded with stars are dark blue or violet, with a green tree. Now there's a painting of night without black. With nothing but beautiful blue, violet and green, and in these surroundings the lighted square is coloured pale sulphur, lemon-green. I enormously enjoy painting on the spot at night. In the past they used to draw, and paint the picture from the drawing in the daytime. But I find that it suits me to paint the thing straightaway. It's quite true that I may take a blue for a green in the dark, a blue lilac for a pink lilac, since you can't make out the nature of the tone clearly. But it's the only way of getting away from the conventional black night with a poor, pallid and whitish light, while in fact a mere candle by itself gives us the richest yellows and oranges. I've also done a new portrait of myself, as a study, in which I look like a Japanese. You never told me if you had read Guy de Maupassant's Bel ami, and what you now think of his talent in general. I say this because the beginning of Bel ami is precisely the description of a starry night in Paris, with the lighted cafés of the Boulevard, and it's something like the same subject that I've just painted now.

Speaking of Guy de Maupassant, I find what he does really beautiful, and I really recommend that you read everything that he's done. Zola – Maupassant, De Goncourt, one has to have read them as thoroughly as possible in order to get a reasonably clear idea of the modern novel. Have you read Balzac? I'm reading him again here.

My dear sister, I believe that at present we must paint nature's rich and magnificent aspects; we need good cheer and happiness, hope and love.

The uglier, older, meaner, iller, poorer I get, the more I wish to take my revenge by doing brilliant colour, well arranged, resplendent.

Jewellers are old and ugly too, before they know how to arrange precious stones well. And arranging colours in a painting to make them shimmer and stand out through their contrasts, that's something like arranging jewels or – designing costumes.

You will see now that by regularly looking at Japanese prints you'll enjoy making bouquets even more, working among flowers. I must finish this letter if I want it to go off today. I shall be very happy to have the photograph of our mother that you mention, so don't forget to send it to me. Give my warm regards to our mother; I often think of you both, and I'm really pleased that now you know our life a little better. I really fear that Theo will find himself too lonely. But one of these days there will be a Belgian Impressionist painter, the one I mentioned above, who will come to spend some time in Paris. And there will be many other painters who will soon come back to Paris with their studies done during the summer.

I kiss you affectionately, and Mother too.


Ever yours,
Vincent

**VAN GOGH'S CORRESPONDENCE: CITATION AND TEXTS OF LETTERS**

The first number in the captions refers to the numbering in the most complete and recent Dutch edition of Van Gogh's correspondence, *De brieven van Vincent van Gogh*, ed. H. van Crimpen and M. Berends-Albert, 4 vols., The Hague 1990. The second number refers to editions in other languages, including English.

For the quotations from Van Gogh's letters, the translator has relied both on previously published translations and on the new translations, as yet unpublished, made by the Van Gogh Letters Project team of translators, who have worked from new transcriptions of the Dutch letters. The translations of letters on pp. 82-93 are translations originating from the Van Gogh Letters Project. This project, launched in 1994 by the Van Gogh Museum in collaboration with the Huygens Institute in The Hague, includes extensive research into all the original letters written by and addressed to Vincent van Gogh. The ultimate objective is a complete edition of the letters, both in their original languages (Dutch and French) and in a new English translation, which will be accompanied by detailed commentary and illustrated with works of art by Van Gogh and other artists mentioned in the correspondence. This edition will be published in its entirety on the Internet and also, in several volumes, in book form in 2009.

**LITERATURE**

Editions of the letters:

- *The complete letters of Vincent van Gogh*, 3 vols. Introduction by V.W. van Gogh; preface and memoir by J. van Gogh-Bonger. Boston etc. (Little, Brown and Company) 1991.
- *Letters of Vincent van Gogh. A facsimile edition*, 2 vols. Preface by J. Leymarie; introduction by V.W. van Gogh. London (The Scolar Press) and Amsterdam (Meulenhoff International) 1977.
- *The letters of Vincent van Gogh*, ed. R. de Leeuw. London (Penguin) 1996.

Further reading:

- J. Hulsker, 'The letters', in E. van Uitert and M. Hoyle (eds.), *The Rijksmuseum Vincent van Gogh*. Amsterdam (Meulenhoff/Landshoff) 1987, pp. 51-58.
- J. Hulsker, *Vincent and Theo van Gogh. A dual biography*. Ann Arbor (Fuller Publications) 1990.
- J. Hulsker, *Vincent van Gogh. A guide to his letters*. Amsterdam (Van Gogh Museum) 1993.
- *Vincent's choice. Van Gogh's Musée imaginaire*, ed. Chris Stolwijk et al. Exhibition catalogue, Amsterdam (Van Gogh Museum) & London (Thames and Hudson) 2003.

## VAN GOGH IN FOCUS

*Van Gogh in focus* is a series of books, initiated by the Van Gogh Museum in Amsterdam on the life and work of Vincent van Gogh. Although so much has been written about this extraordinary artist, many questions still need to be answered or have been addressed only in specialist publications. These small, compact books will examine the artist's oeuvre in different contexts throughout the various stages of his life. Each book will focus on unusual viewpoints in Van Gogh's art – such as his remarkable paintings of sunflowers, his passionate correspondence, or his deep love of nature – and will present many new facts and insights. The series is fully illustrated with documents, as well as paintings and drawings by Van Gogh.

Already published in this series:
Peter Hecht, *Van Gogh and Rembrandt* (2006)
Louis van Tilborgh, *Van Gogh and Japan* (2006)

For recent information about new and upcoming titles:
www.vangoghmuseum.nl/museumpublications

## ILLUSTRATIONS

Front cover: Sketch in a letter from Vincent to Theo, 28 October 1883 (401/336), Van Gogh Museum, Amsterdam
Title page: Vincent van Gogh, *Still life with a plate of onions*, 1889, Kröller-Müller Museum, Otterlo
Back cover: Letter to Theo, detail, The Hague, c. 1 August 1882 (253/221), Van Gogh Museum, Amsterdam

*Van Gogh in focus* is published under the auspices of the Van Gogh Museum, Amsterdam

Editorial board *Van Gogh in focus*
Chris Stolwijk, Leo Jansen, Heidi Vandamme, Suzanne Bogman

With the collaboration of
Nienke Bakker, Hans Luijten, Michael Hoyle

Head of publications
Suzanne Bogman

Editorial assistant
Geri Klazema

Translation
Diane Webb

Text editing
Michael Raeburn

Production
Tijdsbeeld & Pièce Montée, Ghent
Ronny Gobyn (director)

Coordination
Barbara Costermans, Tijdgeest, Ghent
Hans Cottyn, Tijdsbeeld & Pièce Montée, Ghent
Hannelore Duflou, Tijdsbeeld & Pièce Montée, Ghent

Graphic design
Griet Van Haute, Ghent

Typesetting
Griffo, Ghent

Colour separation and printing
Die Keure, Bruges

© Van Gogh Museum, Amsterdam/Mercatorfonds, Brussels
www.vangoghmuseum.nl
ISBN 90 6153 706 1
EAN 978 90 6153 706 9
D/2006/703/46